Searching For Bate Besong
A Play

Mbuh Tennu Mbuh

Langaa Research & Publishing CIG
Mankon, Bamenda

Publisher:
Langaa RPCIG
Langaa Research & Publishing Common Initiative Group
P.O. Box 902 Mankon
Bamenda
North West Region
Cameroon
Langaagrp@gmail.com
www.langaa-rpcig.net

Distributed in and outside N. America by African Books Collective
orders@africanbookscollective.com
www.africanbookcollective.com

ISBN: 9956-791-71-7

DISCLAIMER
All views expressed in this publication are those of the author and do
not necessarily reflect the views of Langaa RPCIG.

Author's Preface

This play has been in the drawer for a long time – more than a decade – and it has followed me to places, both physically and in my mind; and all this while, rehearsing itself out in various formats. At the start of this formal compilation, I realized that there were about two and a half pages of the typed MS and I then searched in vain for the rest. Then some two years ago, I decided to dig into two of the cartoons in which I still have lots of junk, and behold the original MS was there in four Ngoaekele examination booklets with lots of editing. In the same cartoon I found a draft of what was obviously an article, entitled 'BB in Bonamoussadi', with a second tentative title, 'The Writer as Critic'. The first, which was about two pages of the broullion was re-captioned at the start of the two pages as 'BB in Bonamoussadi … in Search of a New Muse?' Although the causality between this draft (which was later modified in editing to read 'BB in Bonamoussadi: Artistic Constituencies, Political Strongholds and the Anglophone Cameroon Writer') and Searching for Bate Besong is so significant, if only because it properly historicises the consciousness from which the play developed, I have decided not to include it in this preface because it mainly addresses BB's poetic imagination. For the second article draft, seven and half pages of hand-written analysis, there was a single line slanting across each page, a characteristic marker of material which I have already typed. But because I don't have this document in my files, I can only suppose that it disappeared either with a hard drive crash or was damaged in my many floppy disks that were so vulnerable to clumsiness before more sophisticated storage facilities were available.

When I discovered the play MS, I immediately set to typing it, aware too that a posthumous BB aesthetic inevitably invades the final product – thankfully in an enabling way. But I have tried to keep as close to the original MS as possible. Now, I wonder what BB would have made of this play, for it is in many ways a reaction, in the form of a discursive interrogation, also, to his creative approach, as much as a deep-seated confession to its seductiveness. The most protean personality in Anglophone Cameroon literature, if not all of Cameroon literature, BB consciously participated in mythologizing himself and his art, an endeavour that made him rather aggressive toward contrary views. Whether we see this as a flaw or not, the important thing is to realise that BB possessed that rare instinct to self-awareness that was so strong it tended to manifest as arrogance. Even condescension can be a mark of the realist's confidence, and BB never waited for others to trumpet his merits: he went ahead of his readers and critics and tried to determine the ways in which he and his vision could and should be accommodated. And we know that he was not always right because, after all, he was only human. In writing BB then, I am also adjusting my own engagement with his challenging aesthetics, for is criticism not another way of offering alternatives, resolving nuances, even if in the process we pattern new controversies?

This may also be a final admission that the controversial icon of Anglophone Cameroon Literature and Criticism has finally been put to rest in my mind. For, about a week or so before the launch of the Disgrace collection of poems, BB emailed me about the event, and suggested the possibility of a review from me. So, from my ntang in Robin Hood country where I was trying to demystify another cultural iconoclast, D. H. Lawrence, postcolonially, I called a cousin in Buea and arranged with him to mail a copy of Disgrace to me. But, helas! The following morning he instead called to find out if I'd heard the ghastly news! It took me two years before I could muster the courage to delete BB's number from my phone; somehow, I'd entertained a hope that one day, he was going to call and say we've all been dreaming about his – and the others' – demise. So now, I find my peace...

My worry over the nature of the Besongian personality, and how it is mediated in his writing, even when I used to chat with BB, was always complex in itself to define: which BB are we dealing with? (Notice that I insist on the present tense). In other words, it was very easy to sit with one BB and be talking with another, wherein disagreement became inevitable because a third often intruded into the conversation, castigating fraternities of barely a few minutes before. The very BB who would shout – that's how he generally conversed even when he thought he was whispering – and wanted to find out from me, because I was not there, if 'Nkengasong told you – did he? – that I took the battle to the enemy; and told them that Anglophone Cameroon li-te-ra-ture is a pa-trio-tic li-te-ra-ture! (the words came out of his mouth as verbal chunks of his own emphatic emotions)' – this fiery presence, stuttering vowels into devastating consonants for violent semantic intent, would neutralise every critical opinion of this literature that did not premise him or his ideological stance; and then rage into denunciations of what he considered 'numbskull intellectuals' who engaged in 'collegiate criticism', even as he himself seduced such accolades; although to be fair to him, he shunned mediocrity without a shadow of pretence. But he was also very romantic in a unique way (glimpses of which are celebrated in The Grain of Ngom Jua); and would shout emotional confessions to his lady across a busy Yaoundé street like a twenty-first century courtly lover whose heart was bleeding with ancestral balms of unreciprocated love! The problem was that the man himself did not realise this complex personification and often expected people to assess him as per his own momentary estimations. In the presence of BB, you could find yourself negotiating meteorological spaces in Dibuncha and Kouseri at the same time, confounded with extremes of emotions that seemed to be surging from a deep well of the human unconscious.

The question may then arise, already alluded to: which BB am I then concerned with here? Simply put, I am engaged in a search that brackets the critical and creative insinuations of BB's oeuvre within and beyond a constituency that he identified with so passionately. For, he was a patriot-poet whose friendships were hinged on a functional definition of patriotism; one in which individual, social, and geographical locales blended as intimately as they resisted osmotic tactics. In a context where the concept of the patriot is hailed only in speeches and sometimes crass policy, for instance, it is easy to understand BB's aversion to the characteristic doublespeak of ceremonial patriots; that is, those who pronounced the word 'patriotism' with water in their mouths and often do so in cine-space. In his rage, on the other hand, BB would pronounce it like a thunder clap from the Fako, and dare anyone to contradict him! And because every healthy criticism is itself contradiction at best, I engage with BB's 'world' as a means of taking the debate to a different stage. It is an interaction that implicates me (and hopefully my reader) in the reading, analysis, and valorisation of his worldview, together with my biases for and against this, mainly because in criticism, as in our opinions of others, we admit to our own perceptions, and how, given the opportunity, things could be reimagined.

We read him then, as I endeavour to do in this play, as representative of our own fears and aspirations, in the hope to fill-in the blank spaces of our chequered and patronised history; we read him to see a version of where the rains started beating us, in the hope that we may finally begin to understand too what it means to be a patriot in a composite way, away from the characteristic distortions by those who have been described as 'bright minds that [lecture] the rest of the nation [through] a lot of intellectual posturing and historical revisionism'. The anger and the insults, the controversies and contradictions that so define BB are all spices to the enabling psyche that left us with a very fertile reservoir from which we can prospect the future for what it is or should be.

From conversing with, reading, and writing about BB, I have come to realise that ethical responsibility threatens every supremacist or differentiating utterance that attempts to arrogate the right of vision. And we – including BB – are so vulnerable when it comes to this simplistic authentication. But there may be an explanation. Caught in the man-made storm of what he saw as 'climates of colossal gullibility', BB seemed to have imagined that Moses could succeed in having a priceless view of the Promise Land only by staging reaction after reaction against an apparently crippling immanence. As part of the writer's responsibility, the ethical paradigm, which we try to understand, from BB's perspective, can be better expressed from the Nietzschean motto that, 'what is done out of love always takes place beyond good and evil'. Now, as moral terms, love, good, and evil are also abstracts that always overlap in the same personality, and it is an illusion to argue otherwise since we will only be offering half-personalities. For Nietzsche, good and evil are limiting elements of a more complex human and cosmic personality, which, even as the stepping stone to the realisation of the controversial will-to-power, still validates the basic duality and truth that life in all its forms is never a fifty percent bargain.

I draw on 'love' as used by Nietzsche to argue that part of the problem with our postcoloniality, which BB more than perhaps any of us, seemed to have diagnosed, is a reductionist disposition to the love-idea. It has been transformed into a trivial sequencing of socio-religious mores, whereas in its inelastic purview of possibilities, love acknowledges other sentiments that are conveniently phrased as anathema. It is embarrassing that in a society in which virtually every lip confesses love in its myriad forms, there is still a lot of pain, anger, and frustration; schemed confessions that serve a strategy of conscious discrimination between love's complementary variables, good and evil.

Indeed, BB makes us to realise that every good person is courageous and inspires confidence because he or she is full of love. His/her ideas may be recalcitrant to a self-appointed public moralist like Honourable Fonkhaunashu, but s/he is never intimidated by stereotypes and their aggregate positions. Such a fellow may not be beautiful as the eyes and brains prescribe, but s/he is a beautyful personality as one of our unheeded post-independence town-criers, Ayi Kwei Armah, demonstrated graphically. And s/he does not need to go to the church or the mosque to justify his/her goodness. And the reason is simple: in the protean self, everything fits and adjusts with time and space, and we need to be attentive in transposing this onto a realistic stage.

MTM
Yaounde, March 1, 2014

x

Dramatis Personae

DOCKINTA .... idealistic don; writer

MBANISAH .... an aged journalist

HON. FONKHAUNASHU .... a politician

MAN
MARIYA ⎬ .... Fonkhaunashu's ballot-sheep/
redeemers of the land

SERGEANT .... Fonkhaunashu's real arm

VOICE .... Big Brother's eyes and ears
and nose

The Spark!

The curtains pull apart to reveal a huge auditorium flushed with lights. A table draped in white cloth and three chairs. Only a few rows of seats are occupied mostly by children so that in the vast emptiness, sound is amplified in echoes. DOCKINTA appears at the entrance and is only momentarily taken aback by the vacant hall; he switches on a broad smile and strolls toward the scanty space, bowing at intervals, under the illusion of applause, lifting the folds of his agbada. *But he contemplates the empty seats, continuously shaking his head; then on a sudden impulse turns away and faces the audience and claps his hands for attention, smiling. His comportment should give the impression that the 'stage' audience is exactly the one he is addressing.*

DOCKINTA: Well … good people … well, here we are at last, to celebrate the fruits of my, or let me say, our collective imagination. And I must thank the organisers [*beams on the imaginary group*] for such a marvellous job. [*pause*] I don't know much about launches and luncheons but er… what we are about to witness this evening, ladies and gentlemen, is the baptism of my most recent publication entitled *Fighting in the Dark*. A very ordinary title, I must admit. But while we await the moment for more eloquent speakers to take the floor, I wish for you to consider one small question: what does it imply, fighting in the dark? Or to be more precise, what does it entail? Fighting in the dark … that's the point – there are targets to be marked out in the dark; there are uncertainties to beware of, and certainties to acknowledge; there are the victims to be pitied or not pitied, in the dark; above all there is the responsibility of the *bona fide*, fighting in the dark, to succeed. Responsibility that is hinged on the hope of victory on the one hand, and the fear of failure on the other. The consequences, whether of fear or of hope, I think, are significant for in them are found the seeds of mass salvation or condemnation from or to darkness. [*pause*] This, in summary, is the issue that I have addressed. For, say what you may, when all is said and done, the truth is that I'm burdened to love this land, and I love it with an abiding love, only that it is not reciprocated. Ah! Repeated stabs of all sorts, against my poor heart in this land of my birth, my lamentation. For, this petering enclave of the world is my abode, and my nib is the sword that scars and scares off its atrocities and at the same time stab the pulmonary vein of its enemies. And I, the lone patriot but misunderstood by kin-enemies of this land, this petering paradise misused, the roots of my nib abused, and why and how can I be quiet? Truth is the burden that would slay me if I rehearse the gangster patriotism of her enemies. And I say it without fear or apology then, that it is my only true baptism into humanhood, the pride of my calling. No, I make no apology as far as that goes! [*shrill blast of whistle off stage and sound of rushing feet;* DOCKINTA *appears to be unawares*] Perhaps you wish to know my personal opinion on the small matter of fighting in the dark… [*paces briefly*] I tell you, fighting in the dark is no good; only cowards and heroes of opportunism fight in the dark. We are under lights now; I can see from your faces who is light-complexioned and who is not; I can also see who has fattened jowls and pointed cheek bones; bulging stomachs and long necks …simply because we are under light: lights show us breeders of falsehood, x-rays them, such worshippers of falsehood. [*more alien sounds from off-stage;* DOCKINTA *pauses only briefly*] Truly I tell you, falsehood has now become our national religion. [*harsher sounds off-stage: 'Big-mop Mokolo Dockinta! … fédéralisé-le! … faut Dockinta!'* DOCKINTA *continues, gravely*] I hear you well, but I've known my fate already, so why should I cringe? We can hide our identities as long as we fight and kill and loot in the dark, but with a flash of light, we know ourselves and can identify our targets more accurately. Thereafter, we can arrange the crosses, each on a mound of ground, for the tigers in sheepskin before I submit to the nails sinking through flesh. Listen to me then, for I tell you again, darkness is the coward's constituency where nation-building is the excuse for the muscling of patriots.

[*there is a sudden stampede of feet at the entrance.* DOCKINTA *stops; turns round as a group of masked men rush at him and bundle him up. They struggle; he is finally overwhelmed and is being dragged out. Turns his head toward the audience, briefly*] We are under light, I tell you again and again! And remember that you can never kill it or substitute it with brimstones of fear! Light …light!! [*he is gagged and pulled out. Lights out*]

The Blaze...

Scene I

Some two weeks later. DOCKINTA, *dressed in a colourful* jumpa *and* salah *and skull-cap to match appears on stage – which is just as in previous scene – a brown folio clapped to his chest and a fibre bag slung over his left shoulder. He glances at his watch and then looks around, alarmed. Then he holds the folio between his knees and makes as if to correct his watch but obviously decides not to; withdraws the folio and advances a few more steps: becomes aware of the audience.*

DOCKINTA: Ah, there you are already! But you are really an unpredictable lot, I tell you. Just imagine that last time I had to wait and wait, and in the end only the hoodlums offered me the sponge with vinegar as the alternative to my life. But never mind; all of that is spilled milk now. And I've forgiven them so that the good Lord too can look kindly on them. [*reflects*] But to think that I've been crucified in this place time out of count and I refuse to die! And yet there's no anger in me because I'll not satisfy them that way. I defy their shallow mind-graves into which every good seed is diseased, even as I often tremble at my own self-righteousness. So I forgive them and forgive their progeny too, even as they know what damage they've done to me and my progeny. And looking at you folks, I feel the hand of God on my stabbed heart, healing, and what happened a couple of weeks ago is history. All what is important is that between then and now you have all transformed into the Biblical watchers. [*pauses as shouts are heard from a distance, off-stage*] You get that frenzy? That's exactly the meaning of sabotage! Otherwise, why have they scheduled their rally to coincide with our show? I'm reliably informed that they obtained no authorisation even as I had to go through the needle-eye of our chronic bureaucracy to have one. [*shouts repeated; DOCKINTA lowers the bag to the floor and mops his face with a white handkerchief; glances at his watch*] But have faith; it's our only shield against back-stabbers under hood. With faith you can walk on planted needles and swallow glowing Bakingili coal. That's what I told myself when they locked me up in a rats' fattening kingdom. [*footsteps are heard off-stage, with suppressed coughing*] Ah, they are here at last! …Hey, boys, hurry up …you're already late. [*silence; he edges toward the entrance. Coughing repeated*] Who is there? Any members of Vision Production out there? Speak out for God's sake!

VOICE: [*off-stage*] I am the voice that walks the … [*coughs*] the mined paths of the land. I pinch secrets from steel hearts. You'll not be warned a second time…

DOCKINTA: I see …But we still don't know you!

VOICE: [*as before*] Never mind. I'm always known in due time when renegades submit. [*coughs*] Beware of final submission in the kingdom of rats.

DOCKINTA: I have never been scared of husky voices from the dark. Let the man who feeds on darkness be choked by its rot; I have my faith. [*turns away, to the audience*] I'll love and worship you all till the day you begin to dine in the dark. [*with sudden anger*] And to imagine that these are the very voices of corrosion, which seek to erode the lining of our hearts and brains! [*paces about restlessly*] They pray at the St. Nicodemus Cathedral in the morning and crawl into *marabout* hideouts in the evening. [*calmer*] I'll never respect them till my last drop of blood is sucked away. That's what I told them straight in their stinking faces, even while they administered horror to my soul ... Look at my palms ... see; these are the marks from their cigarette burns ...and these zebra stripes on my back and belly [*lifts his* jumpa *and indicates, turning round; reminisces*] O, such sugarless cups of morning coffee administered from the inspiration of death; and yet the patriot's abused song – my country to love and cherish and protect, amen... [*looks at his watch, suddenly conscious*] How time flies! It seems the others will never come now, with those husky voices of darkness lurking the vicinity. [*brightens, suddenly inspired*] But I have an idea! A few volunteers, please ... it is easy. Who opts, please, it's simple... [*claps his hands to attract attention*] Who'll ride on the wagon? [*indicates a man in the front row*] You, Sir? No?...I knew; I secretly mistrusted your fidelity, in any event, at the moment of reckoning. But I can't do it alone! [*notices a raised hand from the audience; incredulous*] You? This is fascinating! So many strong muscles sitting in resignation to watch wasted limbs such as yours on stage? ... Please make way ... yes, come up ... here, give me your hand. [*takes volunteer's hand and pulls him onto the stage*] Good ... this is a good start, if nothing.

Any more volunteers? [*shrugs, to new-comer*] Well, two is a crowd where there was only one. You can call me Dokinta [*regards volunteer*] Er ... let me see ... Mbanisah – yes, Mbanisah – what role will you play?

MBANISAH: [*alarmed*] Play role and not give you a hand anymore?

DOCKINTA: [*pats him on the back, to assure*] Exactly, that's what you'll do, man ... give me a hand, play a role, see? Dilly-dally kind of thing or egg and chicken *kata-kata*, if you like.

MBANISAH: I'll rather it were a hand ... roles are too definite in this system and can result in burnt fingers.

DOCKINTA: Well, the choice is yours. Life-changing decisions are hatched in a second and very often it doesn't matter when you choose to take them.

MBANISAH: You misunderstand me. I only mean that I have my work, you see?

DOCKINTA: Tell me, Mbanisah, does it matter?

MBANISAH: O yes, like hell it does! And my name is not Mbanisah; I hate wrangles anywhere, Sir!

DOCKINTA: That makes two of us! And it takes at least two to tango. As a matter of fact, if only you wish to know for instance, I abhor those who stage goodness in the name of Christ, such fellows whose credentials describe a hidden agenda, and they tout God and goodness as a smokescreen for dangerous scheming. And when I talk they call me unbeliever, infidel, an enemy of the land; whereas I tell you verily, they are the obnoxious enemies in the house who need to be exposed!

MBANISSAH: Still, in my profession tags are as ingenious as they are dangerous, if in the process you deem it necessary to step on the imperial toes of authority.

DOCKINTA: [*paces about, in reflection; stops, to* MBANISAH] I see ... yes, I really do. But you're only afraid of risking what you don't have. The name and job don't belong to you.

MBANISAH: How, how are they not mine? Look, you'll make me begin to hate you!

DOCKINTA: Okay, man, don't scream. Listen, the name is somebody else's and you'll annoy nobody with it. At least I don't, using mine. Then the job is yours only as long as your boss thinks so. The mark sheet can be a terrible crucifix!

MBANISAH: [*stubbornly*] Then I must seek to please him while I can.

DOCKINTA: [*turns away from* MBANISAH, *feigns anger*] Go away then and please him. To every man his cross. Why should the lean fellow respect the fattened pal? But then remember that men part ways at the grave. [*sits on a chair and appears to be in deep thought.*

MBANISAH *does not move;* DOCKINTA *eyes him without admiration*] I saw a blind man once and thought I could lead him across the river ...

MBANISAH: [*protesting*] I am not blind ... can't you see? But you're too young to understand! You only want to make me angry. Treat me fairly ... I'm not blind!

DOCKINTA: [*calmly*] Nor can you see. It's the same thing. Your eyes are wide open but you insist on seeing darkness. You don't respect yourself.

MBANISAH: Okay, all I ask of you is assurance ... for my personal safety and my job of course. I still believe in living by bread first.

DOCKINTA: Let me give you assurance then, and take you for my slave. But tell me, what is your work?

MBANISAH: [*too eagerly*] Oh, in principle, I write my scripts, update them from monitors, read them over and over again, and then go on the air to feed the world.

DOCKINTA: [*nods slowly, regarding* MBANISAH *more keenly*] I see ... I see now. So you're a journalist?

MBANISAH: Sure! And it is not easy, man, at the same job with no annual leave for thirty-three years! [*in a conspiratorial voice*] On the Political Desk you have to swallow your own sputum for fear it irritates those who reside upstairs in many skins! In fact, Hon

10

Nyamfukah is expecting me at the rally this afternoon. I only stopped here for a possible scoop.

DOCKINTA: You don't have to go there [*getting up*] at least not before I baptise you.

MBANISAH: [*backing away*] O Yesus!

DOCKINTA: Just be calm, man. [*grabs* MBANISAH *on both shoulders and stares into his eyes*] It is an ill omen to be impatient at initiation. [*shoves* MBANISAH *aside gently; rummages his bag and brings out two masks. Tries one on his face; it fits. He removes it and hands the other to* MBANISAH] Let's see how this fits you.

MBANISAH: [*not moving*] You don't think I can put such primitive horror on my face?

DOCKINTA: You have to. As a matter of fact, it is necessary. Do you know that the Black man's face is the most amorphous gift from God? It leads him into, and out of temptation, always.

MBANISAH: [*with resolve*] But I still want to live without disguises!

DOCKINTA: You'll have to suffer death first. [*cosily*] But why not try it at least?

MBANISAH: I guess there's no harm in trying. [*takes mask suspiciously, peers at it all over, puts it on; immediately removes*

11

it] Heavens, this will suffocate a man within a second! The foul smell and howling sensation!

DOCKINTA: You don't go to fight a bully with parched groundnuts in one hand; you need a club and a shield.

MBANISAH: What of this then? [*pushes mask into* DOCKINTA's *face*] What's its use in a fight?

DOCKINTA: I see you're going to be a hard case. I mistook you for a vulnerable old-timer, but they're not all men today who have grey hair.
MBANISAH: You only wish to mend things for yourself ... Think of my security and job too!

DOCKINTA: The hunter who has no more bullets must confront the wolf with stones. So you're now Mbanisah, the peacemaker. But stones alone are not enough; you also need a shield.

MBANISAH: Then I'll be saved?

DOCKINTA: Maybe ... depending on the force behind your stone, the trajectory, and of course your shield.

MBANISAH: [*gestures mask*] But I don't like it...

DOCKINTA: Well, let's see ... [*puts mask on* MBANISAH's *face; straps it behind* MBANISAH's *head*] Now the choice is yours, to be or not to be, remember? [*steps back, regards* MBANISAH] You remind me of the dead. And you have the freedom to talk like them.

You can now sing *Okokoriko* while I hold the rope and the bowl. [*puts on his own mask*]

MBANISAH: Boss will skin me alive if he were to see me now!

DOCKINTA: Don't sound so pathetically dependent; your boss knows that ghosts don't bite. You make me want to pity you, which is wrong.

[*knocking offstage*]

Listen, I think they're here! [*to audience*] Get ready for the show, beautiful people...

[*knocking repeated, loudly, brutally*]

Coming, please … just a minute.

[*removes mask, throws it the bag and hurries out toward entrance. MBANISAH becomes aware of audience*]

MBANISAH: [*advancing on stage-edge*] This is awkward; a minute ago I was one of you, with no worries, now I'm fixed in uncertainty. I wish I were not so forward. [*calls after DOCKINTA*] Hey, man, who is there? [*to audience*] What I was saying is, I never approach a crowd unprepared. You may call it a professional habit. [*singing offstage; MBANISAH looks around wildly*] Dockinta? … What's happening out there? [*moves toward entrance cautiously*].

VOICE: When you finish, ready you neck for rope!

MBANISAH: [*backs off, to audience*] I said it, now you see? But I know that voice … I know it, always in whispers, always in whispers!

[*Lights out*]

Scene II

[*Lights come on with the intensity of the previous scene.* MBANISAH *is still standing on the same spot, but now looking toward the entrance.* EPPESSE *enters from behind, drunkenly*]

MBANISAH: [*turns round wildly; recognises* EPPESSE] Massa, am I glad to see you! [*rushes toward him and extends a hand*] But what are you doing here?

EPPESSE: [*steadying himself with an effort; ignores the hand*] Tha's ma queishion to you maen, not tha'm interestid. One caen niver understand why you chieouse odd places. And me searching for you all over the city!

MBANISAH: O, eyes that can't see then? But you know that the demons I shy from are the rehearsals of my repeated crucifixion when I dare utter any unorthodox word or phrase!

EPPESSE: Pure rubbish, maen, to a guy already high on booze! But wha's vis on your face, maen?

MBANISAH: [*unstraps mask*] Same old story about my inadvertent reincarnations; now you can at least believe and bear me witness. But how did you know I was the one?

EPPESSE: [*a bit steadily, sounding sober*] Anonymity is an illusion these days my boy. There are all sorts of gadgets to get to the truth.

MBANISAH: [*meditatively*] As if I didn't know. But the good that we share is our common baptism, and makes us pals in life and possibly death. I know where I stand, and which banner I serve, dipped in the blood of truth.

EPPESSE: Then wha're you doing here? And today of all days, maen, when all roads lead to the Reunification Square, see where you are! Only remember to gag your throat next time you play clown and dream of heroism.
[*staggers out*]

MBANISAH: [*stares after* EPPESSE *for a while; turns back to audience, pained*] Do you now see the plight of my engagements? I don't know who to trust now. [*somewhere a clock chimes half hour.* MBANISAH *dashes for the exit, stops, returns and dumps mask on bag; looks at audience, undecided, then forces a smile*] I must go; you heard his threats.

VOICE: [*from offstage*] Help … help, please!

MBANISAH: [*looks around in alarm*] Dockinta? … Eppesse, are you the one? … Who's there?

VOICE: People in need … people in labour!

MBANISAH: [*uncertain, backs off to far end*] Come in then!
[MAN *and a woman enter. The woman is pregnant and* MAN *supports her along in slow steps*]

16

MAN: Sorry to disturb sir! We come from the village of Bangemba and need your help. Can you direct us to the hospital?

MBANISAH: Is that why you choose to disturb my fruitful engagement with the people?

MAN: That's what everybody tells us. But my wife, sir ... see!

MBANISAH: Okay, just move on; you'll find it on the third street, but I doubt if you'll find even a fly there, everybody directed to the Square.

MAN: Thanks again sir ... but on right or left?

MBANISAH: My God, can't you even reason? Down the street, on the left of course!

MAN: Thank you again sir. You're so kind ... Mariya, come ... [*almost carries* MARIYA *out as she is sinking on her knees*]

MBANISAH: [*walks toward centre stage, to audience*] Disguises, accusations, and now this! That's my fate, never a peace of mind whether in the office or anywhere. For instance, Boss always insists on news updates but will never say if the thing was done or it's the same porridge of a week ago being served a hypnotised people. But he's still the Boss with big book-head, big mouth, and very big stomach, and a red ball-point pen which he won at the last fund-raising bazaar for the Party, and swears the red ink will flush us all into misery the moment the news is poorly updated. He

17

cares for no rules for there are none to follow. That's the fate of all our bosses, if you ask me; they always find themselves in odd hemispheres from where they sign the installation of misery. [*glances at his watch in style, mimics*] Any objection? ... None, so adopted as signed!

VOICE: [*from offstage*] Red ink shall fill the blank spaces of your death certificate before you're through!

MBANISAH: Eppesse! [*to audience*] I thought that voice was too familiar. Please let me go now...

[*turns to go as* DOCKINTA *and* HON ANANIAS FONKHAUNASHU *enter, the latter with a brisk limp. His stomach seems to stretch his shirt to its limits, his broad tie glued to the protrusion with a glittering pin. His pants are undersized, causing the limping walk. He is wearing black goggles*]

DOCKINTA: Hey, rushing off already?

MBANISAH: Why, my whole day is wasted, man.

DOCKINTA: I was struggling to calm down our friend here and assure him that there was no fire in the house yet.

FONKHAUNASHU: [*pushes* DOCKINTA *aside*] I'm no friend of yours, you deceiver! [*to no one in particular*] These are my people indeed! How you're trapped in a foolish world where nothing ever happens except in mirages! But no worry; I'm here to personally set things right. [*makes the sign of the cross*] I thank the Virgin Mother for leading my steps here, to liberate you.

DOCKINTA: Our problem in this land is that we pray too much to the wrong God who doesn't know the path to the shrine.

FONKHAUNASHU: Rubbish of your pagan brain. [*casts a vacant look across the space*] And to imagine that ever since I was reliably informed about your annoying speculations against the visionary course we're pursuing, I've been searching in vain for an imposing personality, whereas you're such a skinny lout!

DOCKINTA: [*unperturbed, calmly*] You've been searching the wrong places and for the wrong signs, Honourable. As long as you keep on doing that you'll never find me even long after I'm gone. How can you expend so much energy and resources searching for yourself? My dreams are your dreams, just like my woes, trials, and tribulations. And to capture me, you have to first handcuff yourself; just like you can't torture me without cringing against the raw pain, and the fear of pain, tearing through your soul. O, miracle of the spirit and the flesh; and of the pound of flesh with or without blood; plus the acknowledged or unacknowledged complementarity that you and I represent, like day and night, good and evil, the mystery of life and death, here and there, you know. Impossibilities are man-made, and take us hostage, when duality eases life eternally.

FONKHAUNASHU: Can't you think of something else to say? [*assuring, to no one in particular*] But now that I'm here, everything will just be paradisal.

DOCKINTA: Exactly what I told you sir! We see what we choose to see and hear what we choose to hear. How we express it makes all the difference.

FONKHAUNASHU: [*not listening to* DOCKINTA] I knew something was dangerously wrong ... the Square was empty. I asked the few people strolling by and indicating the beer crates: 'don't you still love me?' And their response was overwhelming: 'We love you dearly!' No objection to that, I said.

DOCKINTA: [*to* MBANISAH] Don't you think he needs a new name?

FONKHAUNASHU: A new what? With my people? [*thunderous laughter*] Listen my boy. First lesson in politics: you can't lead when you assume false identities. Once upon a time I was a political greenhorn. Even when the people took me for the Messiah himself, I still knew something was amiss; I felt insufficient within me, you know, and for a political aspirant that's not a good omen. So I went to work and refined myself by reading the Master of the calling, to become the package you now have. So you can call me the way my people do – Chief, Honourable Ananias Fonkhaunashu, alias Petit Piment.

[another roaring laugh, mops face vigorously]

DOCKINTA: With your influence on the wane the way things stand, Honourable, following the water project scandal, and given the report of the House Committee on Ethics, why should they still trust you?

FONKHAUNASHU: Trust, you say? Who cares about trust and Committee reports today? Trust is an irrelevant word for our new breed of tested leadership, and who are you to say no when I say yes from the political podium. Just show them the transparent ballot box and see how they rush at it in my favour. Never mind what happens upstairs – in the ceiling, I mean.

DOCKINTA: Then they do so with two hearts and that's not safe.

FONKHAUNASHU: For now it is, if I say so. By the way, who cares whether or not they are prostitutes? Torture a prostitute and she'll never scream as long as you give her thirty pieces. I crave only the final pronouncement, let the Fako vomit its filth thereafter!

DOCKINTA: Isn't it then a national tragedy that empty promises have taken us hostage?

FONKHAUNASHU: Will you shut that your tragic mouth! What's wrong with the people's option if things continue the way they are till thy kingdom come?

DOCKINTA: This is free space; no one is deprived of the freedom of expression *here*, Honourable.

FONKHAUNASHU: Then you clearly underestimate me. My powers go beyond the superlative and defy time and space.

DOCKINTA: We're in a new era, a new atmosphere in which anachronistic attitudes are no more.

FONKHAUNASHU: Exactly! So you finally understand? [*places his suitcase on the table, manipulates it open, brings out a poster and reads*] 'In this new era that we pledge from this podium, human rights violation shall be the watchword!' [*to* DOCKINTA] There, what more can you ask for, after this promise of new air, purified, scented, and even acclimatised from tundra mannerisms!

MBANISAH: Then I need more scope! I need to be liberated!

FONKHAUNASHU: [*shocked, as if seeing* MBANISAH *for the first time*] Enh? More scope and liberated? Since when? That's extremely bad language, out of taste. But tell me, what will you do if I said: take, here I give you ten, fifty, even a hundred liberties? You'll still be my slave whenever I, Honourable Fonkhaunashu, choose.

DOCKINTA: [*steadies* MBANISAH *by the shoulders*] You don't have to believe him, can't you see? You're Mbanisah! [*indicates mask*] Act like Mbanisah, not a slave!

22

FONKHAUNASHUU: A conspiracy, eh? You'll only get stewed in the wrath of your own broth.

[*as he speaks* MBANISAH *picks up mask, straps it to his face surreptitiously*].

MBANISAH: Truth, Honourable, that's the sign of my patriotism.

FONKHAUNASHU: And why do you search for truth when it is always elusive?

MBANISAH: Only in this system, Honourable, where we've stigmatised everything into a single lens. Still like the ant that must seek its abode in the bowels of the Fako I can't give up, see?

FONKHAUNASHU: You, your lot, and this Fako thing even after repeated queries. I know because I've generated quite a few of them behind the scene. What's the problem with you and your lot, man? [*mimics*] Don't you shee vhat your truff sh-tandsh in direct oppotishion to mine? [*in normal voice*] Is that not what the boss told you last time and you pledged to be a good boy thereafter? So what's the use except to bore and confuse mankind in the end?

MBANISAH: Let the people choose then; you do what pleases you and I do what pleases me, and let them choose. The choice is always theirs because they're sovereign.

FONKHAUNASHU: Foolish idealism my boy, that's what it is, very foolish. You can never put the back of Fonkhaunashu the post-independence Amalinze on the ground that way, not in this Kingdom. [*laughs*] You'll both have hell after this.

MBANISAH: Hell is one of only two possible kingdoms beyond known existence, sir.

FONKHAUNASHU: And I'll fuel the flames for you [*notices mask*] Hell, remove that horrible thing from your face! [*struggles with* MBANISAH *unsuccessfully to pull it off*] So it's really true the intelligence I received about you this afternoon? Okay, stuff straw into your throat, else I'll recognise it ten miles off.

DOCKINTA: Blunt intimidation will alienate popular support for you, honourable.

FONKHAUNASHU: I know how to get my victory in spite of your popular support. Another name for popular support is vox populi, and no one has ever ruled successfully on the basis of that constituency of toothless bulldogs.

MBANISAH: Blind oppression!

FONKHAUNASHU: Call it what you may; the international community listens and understands a different language, one that assures them of their permanent interest. I don't care if we remain at the primary level for the next millennium as long as our oil and timber distracts them into defining Human Rights upside down! What you call popular opinion is exactly personal conjecture in my vocab. My desire alone suffices. The people don't need your sexed polls.

MBANISAH: Blind tyranny!

FONKHAUNASHU: You think I'm afraid of anything? Nobody threatens my prerogatives in my constituency and go away with it. After all, I've been delegated by divine authority and will metamorphose into a divine House Speaker soon, thanks to the blessings of His Excellency. I've scratched his back for so long now, you know.

DOCKINTA: [*as if emerging from frozen posture, tableau-like, to heighten the solemn effect of his words, which should contrast* FONKHAUNASHU's *erratic rendition*] What shall you say on Judgement Day, Honourable?

FONKHAUNASHU: [*like a priest*] Why, to those who had, more was added; and for those who helped themselves, the good Lord himself assisted them fifty fold. I'm a neoliberal patriot, and my faith is mine alone.

MBANISAH: [*same mood as* DOCKINTA] And divine curse shall rest on the heads of your progeny.

FONKHAUNASHU: Then that shall be their misfortune. For me, I'm fortunate maybe because my old man never took risks, and that's all that matters.

[*knocking offstage*]

VOICE: [*offstage*] Help please … we're the deprived help-seekers of Bangemba.

FONKHAUNASHU: Then come in ye weary and let's consider, on the basis of your inclination.
[MAN *and* MARIYA *enter as before*]

MBANISAH: [*recognises them*] Didn't I say third street on your left?

MAN: The midwife, Sir, she's not on duty.

FONKHAUNASHU: Ah yes, she's at the Square; loyal head of the medical team, just in case.

MAN: [*rushes to* FONKHAUNASHU *supplicating*] My wife, patron, she is under labour.

FONKHAUNASHU: So where you come from, eh?

MAN: From the village-town of Bangemba, Sah. We farm on one side and have settlement on the other.

FONKHAUNASHU: So I hear. Do you know me then?

DOCKINTA: Don't you see the woman is in pain? Attend to her first.

MAN: Yes, she is sir, since last night … No, sah, sorry!

FONKHAUNASHU: [*cocks his head to one side, appears to think*] So you're part of the bloc that voted against me and then called me names and invoked Holy Ghost fire against me?

MAN: We were not part of the rebellion sah. In fact I told the people that it was not good to turn our back on a son of the soil.

FONKHAUNASHU: Hmm, in that case your best bet will be to return to the village where the old women are really skilled in this matter.

MAN: We need a midwife ... it's a complicated delivery.

FONKHAUNASHU: [*rummaging his pockets*] Let me see ... just because you're my people and I should feel at home in Bangemba if ever I visit ... [*brings out some coins, gives them to* MAN] Here, buy some *alaska* ... the red one tempts pregnant women so much and tickles the little rascal to come for it. That will also cool the pains. I'll make sure sister Odilia attends to your wife immediately the rally is over. [*slumps on one of the chairs suddenly, in thought*]

MAN: Thank you very much sah. Come, Mariya.

[*they go out as before.* DOCKINTA *chuckles and* MBANISAH *is infected*]

FONKHAUNASHU: Shut your tragic traps and let a man think! You think it's easy to lead a stone-head people?

Every miserable second of your life is dedicated to resolving problems. You dip your hand in your pocket and something goes out, one-way traffic. Thank God the national purse has no bottom.

DOCKINTA: [*again erect, religious mode*] In the genesis of time, remember, our land was vast and without name and the darkness of ignorance was upon the face of the void. And so we all said, *let there be light*, and behold there was dawn.

FONKHAUNASHU: [*elated*] Quite true, brother! I love that … we now have light all over the place, even in the most enclaved spots like Furukuma Overside … great strides!

MBANISAH: And we said the land was generous; let each harvest according to their needs.

FONKHAUNASHU: Only a fair consideration; every man must pile according to his desire and ability, yes!

MBANISAH: [*his hands locked behind him, pacing gracefully, his face slightly tilted upward*] The vines flourished and the palms ripened; the cocoa pods dripped nectar as the coffee seeds glistened in ripeness. The children were happy and tomorrow was a riddle of hope.

FONKHAUNASHU: Fantastic! That's why the Farmer's Cooperative of Bangemba went national and within a year leapt into the international arena with base near the Elysée Palace. Countless generations shall feed on its dividends.

DOCKINTA: [*same posture*] But evil ate into the hearts of the parent stems.

FONKHAUNASHU: [*gestures frantically*] No, not that, *kai*! Can't you understand? We merely considered our friends and the many ninety-nine year friendship protocols.

DOCKINTA: And the children die in thousands daily.

FONKHAUNASHU: Sheer parental carelessness, like the couple just gone … simple antidote for pain they don't know; and all our relentless health for all campaigns like water and salt solution that would make cholera history. But they are addicted to munching *kuru-kuru*.

MBANISAH: Because no Thomas should exist beyond the official voice, Honourable.

FONKHAUNASHU: Respect for hierarchy and officialdom, that's all. The sun's rays pour from above, not from below.

MBANISAH: Because today healthy ticks cling to the saps and we are called upon to scratch their shelled backs in patriotism.

FONKHAUNASHU: Moral education: do unto others as you would them unto you, simply.

MBANISAH: Because today we're forbidden to weep when sewage rats rip the national purse from below and we thank God because the national purse has no bottom.

FONKHAUNASHU: Hey, wait a minute, you misinterpret me! Beware of misinterpretations!!

DOCKINTA: [*faces* FONKHAUNASHU, *calmly*] Life is a perpetual repetition of shadows and of the shadows of shadows. Even my own self-righteousness becomes an encumbrance that threatens my very existence! I too don't know myself at times, doubt my own visions, yet I always emerge from the realm of doubt and try to focus. But here, Honourable, we have no more shadows; so we misinterpret nothing.

FONKHAUNASHU: I don't follow you now … come out straight, or you may be soliciting your death.

DOCKINTA: When your eyes lie to your heart because they can no longer blink, what can they not do over the dead who are unfortunate to be living still? When you deceive helpless villagers whose votes legitimise your fraud, why should we expect a new sun?

FONKHAUNASHU: Never say I didn't warn you. But you shall repeat all this in due time.

DOCKINTA: Life is a struggle to live. I struggle every time your clique crucifies me. But you die just once and then live forever.

FONKHAUNASHU: [*laughing*] Foolish illusion, terribly anti-life. Let me live forever *here* where we celebrate eons of abundance and die just once when I have to.

MBANISAH: May you never die, Honourable.

FONKHAUNASHU: Look, this is getting out of hand. Must I continue to be plagued as such?

DOCKINTA: Yes, your rally, Honourable, the hypnotised lot is waiting. And in the aftermath of your neoliberal glee, a national post-mortem shall donate pills of death to the unborn.

[FONKHAUNASHU *glares at him murderously and without a word grabs his suitcase, limps toward door. Lights fade on* DOCKINTA *and* MBANISAH *as they look on. Darkness.*
A bell tolls in the distance.
Lights come up.
FONKHAUNASHU *is in a phone booth talking furiously, making wild gestures, wiping off streaks of sweat from his face with his thumb*]

FONKHAUNASHU: I just said hell, you hear! This is an order, do you hear me? Leave all that … yes, yes, all of them … Jesus, did you ever go to school, mister Officer? Why all these buts and the rest? Listen, my personality is at stake and that of the State too. I'm in the perfect mood to scapegoat any fool. So drop all that ... I don't care whether they are birth, death, or life certificates ... Will you shut up and listen! Be professional and ask no more questions. Just wait outside the theatre when you arrive. This is an order!

[*slams down receiver, breaths heavily. Picks up receiver again and dials a number*]

Hello ... Confidence Chambers? [*warmly*] Ah, frère, how you do na? ... Good, I'm glad to hear that ... sure [*laughs heartily*] But listen, there's some brisk business at hand. Imagine some spineless upstarts who think they can deprive me of my deserved prerogatives! Now, you have to arrange for summary trial ... no, now, not after the elections! That'll boost my ratings ... Don't you worry; I'll supply the facts and then you establish the charges as you deem appropriate ... Of course, your bite! ... Beautiful ... sorry to have bothered you so. Bye!

[*hangs up, breathes deeply, relieved. Picks up suitcase and steps out of booth*]

You only need to know which strings to pull and which buttons to punch in this establishment, and the world will rotate toward you! O, Fonkhaunashu, you rascal!

[*laughs hollowly, heaving himself away*]

Lights out

Scene III

[*In the Amphitheatre. Lights come up and we discover* DOCKINTA *and* MBANISAH *as in previous scene*]

MBANISAH: No, that's not the point; I only wish to know from your formidable brain if we pushed him too far?

DOCKINTA: There's no limit to opposing tyranny. The farther and harder you push, the better. It gets insane with everything and then implodes.

MBANISAH: But the way he left, with blood in his eyes, are we safe?

DOCKINTA: That's part of the game. The cornered tyrant dramatises everything out of proportion if only to hide his inadequacies. The worst part of the drama is by the intellectual politician who is caught between resistant intellectualism and the watery mouth policy of deceit.

MBANISAH: And they're your colleagues, I suppose?

DOCKINTA: Yes, very unfortunate, especially so because it is like the offending finger that I don't know how to chop off even as Christ himself is said to have instructed.

MBANISAH: Still we must fear for the things we hold dear.

DOCKINTA: Without making ourselves slaves to manipulators who exploit such vulnerabilities for political capital. Our tragedy in this Kingdom is that we think of the future only in speeches. It'll never do because speeches alone can never kill a fly or build a dream.

FONKHAUNASHU: [*rushing in*] You liar ... saboteur!

MBANISAH: O, so you changed your mind?

FONKHAUNASHU: Me, never! I never change my mind.

DOCKINTA: A fixed square peg in a fixed round hole. Perfect conservative nightmare, our doom!

FONKHAUNASHU: [*sits on a chair*] Empty words that cannot kill a fly, see? But as you prefer; I'm not a green snake in green grass. But be it as you prefer. [*opens suitcase and shuffles papers in it, as if looking for something*]

MBANISAH: [*regards* FONKHAUNASHU *briefly, to* DOCKINTA] He is threatening us!

DOCKINTA: That should be his cross, not yours. Threats can't kill a lame ant. [FONKHAUNASHU *looks up briefly, shakes his finger threateningly at* DOCKINTA] Honourable should be more concerned now with the threat against his seat.

FONKHAUNASHU: Lose my seat, you mean? You must be joking. Wait and see what miracles I'll perform at the polls after invading every corner of my constituency.

DOCKINTA: That was the ease of the past; today we have educated Fons and Chiefs who should know better.

FONKHAUNASHU: Massa Teacher, teach me no nonsense, you hear? You're talking about Fons and Chiefs who will lick my backside for crumps? I'll drug them with jugs of *manjunga* and fill their robes with bundles of counterfeit. [*seems to remember something and turns back to his suitcase and searches as if he were reluctant to find it*]

DOCKINTA: The appropriate cue to their idiotic motions of support. [*in a mocking voice*] Considering the fact that fowls have developed teeth since the luminary entrance of the prince on the political stage; considering the metamorphosis of double-throat monsters into the pantheon since then; and considering the fact that every builded mansion now trembles on the stilts of cosmetic neglect, as honorary Cyclops watch the coastline, we hereby pledge body and soul as bricks and mortar for the architect's dream. [*in his normal voice, hands in his pockets, pacing about casually, to* MBANISAH] Pah! Absolutely disgusting, this colossal deification of rot and surrender to same. What Honourable needs in my opinion is a new birth of fire. [FONKHAUNASHU *appears agitated, shuffling more papers*] Passive shafts will no longer do.

MBANISAH: Hey, man, be careful; fire go burn you!

DOCKINTA: We all need the fire now. Our present integrity has got to be shattered, all our ideals carted back to the drawing board for consuming fire.

MBANISAH: In other words, historical repetition for a way forward, yes! All our struggles lie in a single, undulating action, the high and the low moments. So the ceasefire holds here for the guns to go off elsewhere, building and destroying and modifying the nation in one unquestionable patriotic breath.

FONKHAUNASHU: [*looks up instinctively*] Despicable liars! Do you mean to say we've been following the wrong drills or prescribing the wrong drug?

DOCKINTA: A little bit of both, Honourable; a childish cacophony mistaken for national pride.

FONKHAUNASHU: And what would you say if I inform you that you've successfully scratched out your grave with your own fingers?

MBANISAH: [*conciliatory*] Hey, he didn't really mean that, Honourable; after all we're only pretending.

FONKHAUNASHU: You call talk of fire pretence? But I warned you, didn't I? … Just listen! [*snaps suitcase open, brings out a small recorder from among the papers at the sight of which* MBANISAH *is ready to pass out.* DOCKINTA *is curious, edges closer.* FONKHAUNASHU *manipulates the buttons, listens, then increases volume.* DOCKINTA's *voice comes across clearly as if over a loud speaker*] 'What Honourable needs in my opinion is a new birth of fire'. [FONKHAUNASHU *stops it savagely, faces the others, a broad grin on his face*] Ha! This is conspiracy! Through pains of fire … but tell me, who fires what, at who, and why? Are you suggesting … but listen [*again manipulates buttons as above and voice of* DOCKINTA *again comes through*] 'Passive shafts will no longer do'. [FONKHAUNASHU *again break in*] Shafts, yes, I know their devastating effect. Cluster bombs, Hiroshima, Hotel Rwanda … *Et tu Brute!* [*stands up with assumed dignity and strides the space between* DOCKINTA *and* MBANISAH, *speaking and turning from one to the other, with airs*] I stand for passive shafts, if shafts at all, and massive liberation from straying ideologies. Why should loyal citizens not carry passive shafts, if they must carry them at all? Let them walk and act passively if they're happy.

DOCKINTA: For decades now, we've lived like passive slaves to a generation oligarchy; slaves whose only art is to smile eternally so that the master should never know the pain they endure.

FONKHAUNASHU: And for countless more decades you shall live on the whims of our ever youthful leadership. The horizon is broad and limitless. [*shakes his head sadly*] I pity you boys; with your own claws you've dug your own grave.

MBANISAH: [*stammers, fearful*] But my Honourable, we only meant to …

37

FONKHAUNASHU: I know ... meant to kiss my backside. No worry, you're only voices from the grave now.

DOCKINTA: [*unperturbed*] Voices from the grave are shafts of vengeance; you die just once and live forever, Honourable.

FONKHAUNASHU: [*puzzled*] What a stubborn way to console oneself. Truth is, you die once and rot forever.

DOCKINTA: The fly that follows the corpse into the grave still believes the feast is eternal.
[MBANISAH *goes out unnoticed*]

FONKHAUNASHU: Say what pleases you. I know what I know, which is indisputable. You're a menace to state institutions. [*sits down, a contented man*]

DOCKINTA: [*bends over* FONKHAUNASHU, *harshly*] Haven't we heard all of this before, Honourable? Paradise of the chosen few ... infallibility of the pathfinder ... falsehood of the masses ... humanisation of the Trinity in enclaved Bangemba because a wobbling ideology is the way the truth and the life? It's a disgusting mental dish overflowing with deceit, Honourable. [*with a sudden move as if to grab* FONKHAUNASHU *by the throat*] And you insist we must remain silent?

38

FONKHAUNASHU: [*backs away, stumbles over; enraged, getting up*] Do you realise what you've just done? I swear you'll pay for this with blood.

DOCKINTA: I no dey chop for your pocket, Honourable, and you know that! I'll not be one of the mental slaves in your constituency.

FONKHAUNASHU: [*recovering, abstracted*] What's the use of talking when it hardly changes the things that are talked about? At the moment of sacrificial atonement, blood redeems all.

DOCKINTA: Change is never a straight line, Honourable, nor a time-scheduled occurrence. We'll soon line you up according to the sizes of your throats and foul pregnancies, no matter how long it takes. You shall be abandoned in the cold vomit of your swindle.

FONKHAUNASHU: You think I don't know what to put in this suitcase when I go to the people? They don't care about anything else.

DOCKINTA: You disgust me again, Honourable. You thrive on the fortunes of the death.

FONKHAUNASHU: But the safest way to exist in a dungeon of hypocritical masses is to be a chameleon. If I must confess, know then that I'm a chameleon.

DOCKINTA: If I must also confess, Honourable, *á propos* of your own confession, then know that I'm an artist and I know the reaches of patriotic responsibility more than any coat-and-tie citizen. And yes, in my moments of painful reflection, I urge myself: 'Slow down man, slow down; for the artist with a ton of words-bomb can very easily be like a trigger-happy red or black beret, if not worse, cutting down lives with crass abandon'. And that'd the difference, Honourable – I still have a conscience, not just mine but that of the community, whereas you've auctioned yours to Ali Baba magicians!

[*knocking offstage. MAN's* voice is heard again]

VOICE: Please help us ... people in desperation ... we're desperate.

FONKHAUNASHU: [*looks around, misses* MBANISAH] Hey, where is your man?

DOCKINTA: So you didn't notice the way he sneaked away, his old bones crackling in retreat obviously because you bred such fear in his poor soul?

[*knocking repeated offstage. MAN's* voice is heard again as before]

MAN: Please ... desperate people in need.

FONKHAUNASHU: Knock and it shall be opened. Just come in ye weary and find rest under Fonkhaunashu, Rock of the community, watershed for the masses.

[MAN *enters with* MARIYA *who is almost collapsing*]

MAN: Sir, we wish to thank you for the *alaska*, but the pain is still there and getting worse ... not so Mariya?

MARIYA: [*moans*] Oh, lay me somewhere ... now! [*glides onto the floor*]

MAN: [*turns from* MARIYA *to* FONKHAUNASHU] The pain Sir, and getting worse.

FONKHAUNASHU: What can I do alone? This business of deliverance is a partnership, a sort of give and take. [*laughs*] But I'm not sister Odi, you know.

MAN: [*to* DOCKINTA] Can't you help us, Sir?

DOCKINTA: [*feigning surprise*] Oh, me? ... I'm not sister Odi, you know.

FONKHAUNASHU: Watch your foul mouth, you! [*to* MAN] Of course you'll soon be relieved; I'm reflecting on your plight for a long term conceptual solution. For the time being, have faith in me and the institutions that I incarnate. Where is your faith?

MAN: But the suffering Sir, it can't wait. [*to* DOCKINTA] Is there no private practitioner around here?

DOCKINTA: *Kai*! You mean those tropical Shylocks in Canaan? They're worse than suicide bombers! [*indicates* FONKHAUNASHU *with gesture of the head*] Your best bet is to consult those who own you and your seeds; you still hold the ballot paper, which he'll sacrifice his soul to grab. He's more disposed to help you.

FONKHAUNASHU: Are you suggesting that I'm negligent? And you think the people care about your big book rubbish?

DOCKINTA: Okay, I concede they don't for now; but they will when the pain and misery of pain persist. They shall remember when you seduced them for their votes.

FONKHAUNASHU: [*laughs suddenly*] I didn't know you were that numb-skulled. I told you I don't have to approach the people. I'll get them through their Fons and Chiefs. It's no miracle boy, just simple arithmetic.

MAN: [*to* FONKHAUNASHU] Yes, Sir, you shall have all our votes even from the dead and unborn for years, even decades to come, we promise. But help us now.

FONKHAUNASHU: Aren't you believers? So where is your faith, my man? Just be patient man, a God-given virtue. Accidents may occur when we rush.

MAN: [*almost prostrating before* FONKHAUNASHU] She's suffering Sir. I feel it. If she dies …

DOCKINTA: [*furious*] Then you do it yourself, if you've auctioned generations for nothing. Look for a table and urge her to push. [*picks bag, slings it over his shoulder as if leaving*]

MAN: She's going to have triplets, something we've never had in Bangemba. So it's very complicated.

DOCKINTA: Sister Odi will never know. It may be a hydra or even a dragon. Nobody is ever certain about pregnancies and deliveries. Even the saviour himself was of uncertain ancestry. Do you remember Nazareth where nothing good ever came from? [*mockingly*] If she dies …

[MAN *looks pathetically from* DOCKINTA *to* FONKHAUNASHU; *the one is unmoved; the latter shrugs in indifference.* MAN *looks on some more, returns to* MARIYA, *supports her head on his lap and gently mops her brow*]

FONKHAUNASHU: [*to* DOCKINTA] You're such a sadist. But you now agree with me that leadership is peril?

DOCKINTA: Of course, and depends on how the rich man whose highway is the eye of the needle, entices the poor man. But professed goodwill is no longer any guarantee today. You're cruel and unjust to those who hail you!

FONKHAUNASHU: Isn't that enough in the name of peace, unity, and progress? Isn't that enough my … [*turns to* MAN *and* MARIYA, *is confronted by their cold, hostile look; immediately turns to the audience*] Isn't that

43

enough my people? [*to* DOCKINTA] It's enough for us, I tell you.

DOCKINTA: That too will depend on how you define the words. You don't make them capsules of illusion for the people to admire while you ram them down their dry throats.

FONKHAUNASHU: But they don't complain.

DOCKINTA: Because you never want them to. You mistake their sheepish gullibility for patriotic militancy.

FONKHAUNASHU: I see, massa book. So what do you propose?

DOCKINTA: Nothing more than that which they themselves desire now. Beware of how you birth change, be it mental, social or communal.

FONKHAUNASHU: All that na foolish talk …

MAN: But we want help, now!

FONKHAUNASHU: [*ignores him; opens suitcase*] Of course we've changed and keep changing.

DOCKINTA: But remain changeless, Honourable. Change in speeches … progress in decrees, and which all amounts to nought.

FONKHAUNASHU: [*closes suitcase angrily*] You're treading on dangerously forbidden grounds! Are our prisons not overflowing with the fruit of change?

DOCKINTA: Oh yes, we incarcerate the wrong fellows for the wrong purpose. In reality we'll never imprison a dog for robbing the State because we know all the sleepy-eyed, God-fearing hounds who sink tunnels into the State coffers. Thank God the purse of state can never be empty.

FONKHAUNASHU: [*pats* DOCKINTA *on the shoulder*] I see you're disgruntled, my boy. That's an ill omen for the future. But if midnight decree breeds noon rumour from gutter, what then? What if we even exterminate your seedy future with a single syringe, even then weti you fit do, eh?

DOCKINTA: The last birth always resurrects the house pillars. We can't be happy under a roof with rotten poles. [FONKHAUNASHU *stares at him, with open mouth*] We need steel rods for reconstruction after which the good intentions of men must flourish.

FONKHAUNASHU: Everybody's intention will only breed chaos, my man. Even your intentions are only intellectual theories on which nothing practical ever grows. Frankly speaking, the people don't need your theories of good intentions. They are the people and will always form the contented majority against your barren intentions.

DOCKINTA: Then they are a majority with no dignity.

FONKHAUNASHU: Beware of the curse of the people, my friend. You'll always be overwhelmed in every bout by …

DOCKINTA: A mob that has been overwhelmed by falsehood.

FONKHAUNASHU: [*triumphal*] But they never know it; that's the miracle!

DOCKINTA: Still they remain the mob and a lethal weapon. I know there's never been a sensible mob in history. We only rationalise its action from hindsight.

MBANISAH: [*coming in, excitedly*] Exactly! When they succeed, they are reapers of passion; but when they fail, they become puppets of mercy. [*notices* MAN *and* MARIYA] Eh-eh, you again?

FONKHAUNASHU: Don't disturb them. Where did you vanish to?

MBANISSAH: Thought of my marksheet and the red pen of Boss.

FONKHAUNASHU: You know you look like a conscientious fellow, when I almost mistook you for one of the disgruntled lice who oppose everything.

DOCKINTA: I met a hungry mob of blind men once arguing on how to get out of a slough. And I said, why not use your staves against the bald-headed fool who led you into the mud so that even if you finally sink, you should have been appeased? But they conferred and instead decided to use their clubs on me. I stood on the bank and watched as they were almost choking to death.

FONKHAUNASHU: You're a very poor storyteller. I can beat you at it any time.

DOCKINTA: There are poor storytellers and incompetent liars. [*indicates* MARIYA] That's evidence of incompetent lies telling, Honourable; she's your cross, not mine, so don't try to hang it on my neck.

FONKHAUNASHU: [*with firmness*] Is that so? Okay, then be ready for what you've brought onto your exposed head!
[*rushes out as lights too go out*]

The Smoulder

Scene IV

[*Faint light showers the stage.* DOCKINTA *and* MBANISAH *are gathered at the entrance stretching the necks to see.* MARIYA *has fallen asleep, supported by* MAN. *Lights gradually flush the whole stage*]

FONKHAUNASHU: [*offstage, to someone*] That was the last straw and for how long can we continue to spare the rod of State? And what do they really want? That I visit their enclaved spots ... bring them rain in the dry season ... bring forth their little rabbits and disfavour myself in all that. So you just rush in at my signal, you hear? [*appears at entrance;* DOCKINTA *and* MBANISSAH *retreat*] Prepare yourselves for the last act, gentlemen. Gethsemane is here at last.

MBANISAH: But you didn't have to take us seriously; we were merely make-believing!

FONKHAUNASHU: What do you take me for, eh? What will the people take me for, after this?

MBANISAH: I've already taken care of what they'll take you for, Sir; I was just from the newsroom.

FONKHAUNASHU: [*eagerly*] Tell me, now, what did you say?

MBANISAH: The scripted oration to the benevolent hypnosis that you incarnate, Sir.

FONKHAUNASHU: Aha! Fire, my boy! Beautiful phrase! O, you patriot!

MBANISAH: [*in a newscaster's voice, deliberately faltering*] His very Excellency the Minister of State for National Enrichment and Member of Parliament for the Kamtok Region, has revealed government plans for unlimited prosperity of that national enclave in the aftermath of the present political consultation. [FONKHAUNASHU *nods repeatedly*] Speaking at a rally this evening at the Tribulation Square that was attended by over fifty thousand supporters and sympathisers …

DOCKINTA: That's a bloody lie!

FONKHAUNASHU: And so? It's his job … fire on my boy!

MBANISAH: [*unruffled*] … the man of the people disclosed that according to projections from the database of a French company that deals with rabies in tropical cats, and in accordance with the magnanimous prescriptions of Party think-tank on rural exodus and revitalisation of the primary sector of our economy …

FONKHAUNASHU: *O, la la!* Does it not sound like a piece of verse from paradise! [*suddenly embraces* MBANISAH] Ah, Comrade, Camarade, Compatriot!

Little tributaries forge the nourishing ideology in the armpit of the Atlantic. Strange, but this reminds me of that historic speech I delivered almost a decade ago to the representatives of the people of Bangemba here in the capital, remember?

[*lights suddenly fade on stage and in the dimness the scene changes into a sensitization campaign with ideologically fitting banners and posters.* FONKHAUNASHU *mounts the rostrum adjusting his tie consciously. He is now wearing glasses, and sports a beard and a Party scarf knotted around his neck. All through the address, he should appeal with appropriate gestures; while the other characters on stage cue in as representatives of the population. Clears his voice importantly before speaking*]

On behalf of our Very magnanimous Chairman who sends you his very considered benedictions, make I salute all of you, people of Bangemba, here-assembled! [*ululatory shouts echo through the loudspeakers*] Make I also take this rare and God-given opportunity to thank all wouna plenty for coming all this way like true children of the fatherland in order for hail the ideas of we great party. Make wouna continue with this kind of patriotic and unflinching support for Party and Government not necessarily for what you have but for the things that are to come. Reward go come with time, I assure you because Government's time is the best! I can also assure you that when the roads are good I'll personally pay you a deserved visit in return for your present gesture [*in the absence of the expected ululations, coughs importantly; sips from his glass*]

MBANISAH: [*waving affirmative placard*] We want good road like the one for capital.

FONKHAUNASHU: [*smiles broadly*] Aha, war don start! [*laughs hootingly*] Let me tell you small secret. For ask question no bad at all, but the best thing is to have confidence in the leadership you elected overwhelmingly. [*addressing* MBANISAH] My man, you think say we no know about this bad fever for outside called economic craze? Make man no lie you! And I tell you true, we even want escape from capital come meet you for Bangemba because all kind rubbish and cholera don capture capital. [*mixture of applause and laughter over speakers*] Yet, I know that you cannot comprehend the full magnitude of this economic demon [*cheers and applause*] … You can't because Bangemba people na a very hard working lot. I hear say wouna motto na "NO FOOD FOR LAZY MAN". Absolute patriotic truth! Dat's why wouna faces di always shine like dem rub'am with minyanga oya! [*hooting laughter from* FONKHAUNASHU *amidst wild applause*] So continue for work farm well, plant more food, maintain existing roads, build more classrooms and born many more children who will become new builders of the nation when we retire. That na proper self-reliant development.

DOCKINTA: [*with plebeian misery*] We want health centre too!

FONKHAUNASHU: Excellent suggestion! But to get your health centre, first build Party House so we fit take good decisions inside about the location, cost, tender, and contributions from you the militants. I know that Bangemba people all over the fatherland na very dynamic and hardworking militants. But good militant must first buy card and pay dues promptly.

MARIYA: Add money for coffee and cocoa, Sah!

FONKHAUNASHU: Truly, I share your concern, my sister. Na true say prices don tumba. But let me assure you that Party and government officials hardly sleep because of your anxiety. But as prices are down we encourage wouna for increase quantity. In the end you go still be rich, no be so?

MAN: Price don fall, make tax too fall Sah!

FONKHAUNASHU: That kind thing no fit ever happen, my good friend [*protesting voices shouting 'WHY? WHY?*] That go make we come out of fry pan only to fall for fire! Govmen go loss plenty. Secondly that na very bad economic planning, with no future. Thirdly, na wouna Bangembans be the backbone of the economy. We for capital no even get kobo for buy petrol but wouna get the real petrol for belly. We jealous wouna too much! [*applause and laughter*]

MBANISAH and MARIYA: [*severally*] We want clean water … We want iletrik too and college.

FONKHAUNASHU: Very good then. I don hear. When I hear na Party do hear; when Party hear, na govmen don hear. When govmen hear, wouna go surely get plenty. Wouna fit even get everything. Just give us your support and time.

DOCKINTA and MAN: [*severally*] We support Party and govmen … We support you too.

FONKHAUNASHU: I thank wouna plenty. Already, govmen don grant gendarme post for next budget. Big prison go follow so that nobody can disturb your peace. [*applause*] After that treasury go come for guard against any financial mishap. As for church wouna get more than enough for last till Papa Jesus Christ come back. Then pipe-borne water and electricity fit follow [*thunderous applause*] Immediate results, that's what we stand for. So I leave wouna – or better still, wouna leave we for capital – with two important sayings. The first na for love your neighbour as yourself; so no more para-para and petitions. The second na say, the fear of our leader na start of wisdom. So report any recalcitrant mind plotting against his image. Thank you very much. And long live we fatherland!

[*sustained applause. FONKHAUNASHU waves and light fade out. Stage again returns to previous state. FONKHAUNASHU turns to DOCKINTA and MBANISAH as full lights return. MAN and MARIYA are still huddled together as if asleep*]

So gentlemen, that's the record I set in the history of political speech-making with the resulting 99.99% at the polls. That's also why I'm on the road once again.

DOCKINTA: Repent ye then, O sons of man, for the caravan of salvation is cruising by!

FONKHAUNASHU: Indeed, and what else can I say!

DOCKINTA: Times are changing O daughters of God. Hurry and reap your share before the vultures alight.

FONKHAUNASHU: [*stares at* DOCKINTA] What do you mean now? That's distorting the gospel!

MBANISAH: [*with a comic leer*] In the final act of clemency deprived sons shall clutch swords against fathers and daughters wield clubs against silent and silenced mothers before the birds swoop ... ha, ha, ha!

FONKHAUNASHU: You too? You're crossing carpet, you traitor!

MBANISAH: Names no longer kill, otherwise many would have long moved on, Honourable.

DOCKINTA: In the final hour of agony, the end and the beginning, parents shall be pushed into dry flames by claws from the womb.

MAN: [*looks up suddenly, shaking his head*] We want relief now ... my wife ... Mariya ... was I dreaming?

DOCKINTA: Today, desire without will is deadly sin. The spirit must will heavy flesh along!

MAN: [*springs to his feet and rushes at* FONKHAUNASHU] My wife needs deliverance! [MARIYA *moans*]

FONKHAUNASHU: [*pushes MAN away; adjusts his lapels*] Get off me, you beast of no nation! Must I be plagued by every swine?

DOCKINTA: Beware of the fellow you chase and kick, and he stumbles and falls … stumbles and falls for too long.
[MARIYA *sends out prolonged moan, stretches in fits. Simultaneous sound of a loud bang in the distance, offstage*]

MAN: [*grabs* FONKHAUNASHU *again*] We need a saviour, can't you understand!

[*another bang, offstage*]

FONKHAUNASHU: [*frightened, to no one in particular*] What's that noise? [*weakly, to* MAN, *breathing heavily*] I said let go of me, akunyam! [*frees himself; mops his face*]

DOCKINTA: [*closing in on* FONKHAUNASHU, *as* MBANISAH *does same*] What do you expect of a man you bask in party sun and pelt with ideological stones for too long?
[FONKHAUNASHU *is really frightened now, looks from one person to the next and then at the entrance*]

MAN: Yes, what else do you expect of a man you chase and chase and he runs and falls, runs and falls, for too long?

FONKHAUNASHU: [*darts away with surprising speed toward entrance*] Conspiracy against the Trinity of State, Leader, and Institutions! Sergeant! Come now!!

[SERGEANT *enters briskly, halts, and salutes stiffly.* MAN *backs off to* MARIYA. DOCKINTA *and* MBANISAH *look on stubbornly*]

SERGEANT: A vos ordres, Honourable!

FONKHAUNASHU: You now crawl away like the very cowards you are? You think I'd blunder into your den without my back-up plan? [*to* SERGEANT, *pointing*] Get them! [SERGEANT *draws pistol, rushes first at* MAN *who lifts one hand in surrender and protects* MARIYA *with the other*]

MAN: [*still cuddling* MARIYA] Mariya, Mariya … get up … sorry Sah … surrender Chef!

FONKHAUNASHU: [*kicks* MAN *in the back*] Speak again you intransigent fool and renegade!

DOCKINTA: [*calmly*] Who is the real traitor amongst us, Honourable?

FONKHAUNASHU: [*spins on his heels, slaps* DOCKINTA *savagely*] You of all can never pass judgement on me.

I'll make you swear allegiance to our Idea at gun point [*crouches a bit and stares at* DOCKINTA *in the face*] The length of your rope is now out, let your theories save you [*to* SERGEANT] Get him too; he's the ringleader. [SERGEANT *strides toward* DOCKINTA, *nudges him with pistol toward* MAN]

DOCKINTA: Ringleaders are patriots in history books. You can't help to change the course of the river and hope to plant new fig trees as boundary markers for ever.

FONKHAUNASHU: Fool, and a disgrace to your fatherland! Sponsored evil has eaten into your heart chambers and you are just an empty vessel, the personification of failed patriotism.

DOCKINTA: Ah, listen to your own barren words, Honourable, falling on rock and bramble!

MARIYA: [*stirs awake, then cringes suddenly, distracting them*] Aeeii! The pain … coming now!
[SERGEANT *looks confused, bends over* MARIYA *who seems to lapse back into previous state*]

FONKHAUNASHU: Sergeant! [SERGEANT *straightens up, another stiff salute*] Now clear up the mess.

SERGEANT: [*hesitant*] Pardon, mon Honourable … je ne comprends plus …

FONKHAUNASHU: Not comprends what plus? [*walks up to* SERGEANT *menacingly*] You are not paid to understand anything, but to act!

SERGEANT: But according for règlements dem …

FONKHAUNASHU: Whoever put it in your skull that this is a matter of principles? Arrest them and stop blubbering rubbish about what you have no clue about. Or are you suddenly ambitious? If you need recommendations, you know I'm always your man. But you have to execute orders first.

DOCKINTA: Even the clay of creation is not always a flexible block of earth, Honourable, especially when things are unstable.

FONKHAUNASHU: [slaps DOCKINTA across the face] How he acts damn well depends on who is ordering him. And because I represent the godhead I also determine when things are stable.

DOCKINTA: [offers his hands, held together, to SERGEANT] Go on then and re-enact the ritual of how the Black man was crucified by a coat and tie leadership after what we thought was a Caucasian nightmare. We were ready a long time ago, only that it also took you so long to come, searching for us through the shadows of your own making.

[SERGEANT looks from one to the other of the three; turns toward MAN and MARIYA who are cuddled away in fear, the one watching and the other moaning]

59

FONKHAUNASHU: [*stamps around in fury*] Go on na, or you expect me to do your job for you? Where your chains? Unleash them now!

SERGEANT: Honourable, I think that ... la femme ...

FONKHAUNASHU: You think nothing; I do all the thinking. [MARIYA *suddenly sits up with a start, stretches in slow motions; confers with* MAN] Bring out the handcuffs!

SERGEANT: I forget them for bureau, Honourable ... You no ask for me to bring them; only pistol.

FONKHAUNASHU: How then do you expect to apprehend such recalcitrant elements? [*with self-pity*] Oh God what is happening to me! ... What's going on here? [*suddenly inspired, energised*] Blast them then! Blow away their unnecessary brains!

DOCKINTA: We die just once, remember? But even the fastest runner can never skip his allotted spot.

FONKHAUNASHU: Shurrup there! You pull down every bridge I construct, scatter every ridge I hoe, and yet expect happiness! You'll soon be history and your brother may be spared for now to read the obituaries with his at the end.

SERGEANT: La radio à prit feu, Honourable. Sorry I forget to tell you before!

FONKHAUNASHU: [*dumbfounded*] W-H-A-T?

SERGEANT: Radio don catch fire, Honourable!

FONKHAUNASHU: The most reliable voice of the people? [*grabs* MBANISAH *by the collar*] What happened? You were the last to go there.

MBANISAH: The place was already cordoned off by the time I arrived and no one was allowed to go in. The flames were raging toward the fuel station in the premises.

[*they all stare at* MBANISAH; *even* DOCKINTA *shakes his head approvingly*]

FONKHAUNASHU: Then … then … the news and report of the rally … how did you manage it?

MBANISAH: The way I'm expected to, Honourable. [*taps his head with forefinger*] Here, in my head, specially for you.

FONKHAUNASHU: What do you mean? Has your head become a studio of the Voice of the People?

MBANISAH: Is that not what you wanted to hear? So I read the news here to you from habit.

FONKHAUNASHU: Lord, I'm undone by a creepy, self-seeking, and godforsaken bunch of idiots! May the devil take your entire generation hostage till thy kingdom never, never comes!

[*Seems to realise his situation in a flash; grabs suitcase, takes long strides toward the entrance.* MAN *suddenly gets up, bars his path.* FONKHAUNASHU *regards him with what can be described as ferocious anger;* MAN *does not budge, beckons on* MARIYA *who struggles to her feet and approaches* FONKHAUNASHU *with slow, measured steps as if in a dream, sleep-walking, a cynical smile on her face and her eyes bright;* FONKHAUNASHU *stares at her protruding stomach as if it were a nightmare; lights fade to a lurid glow*]

MARIYA: Sacrifice, now!

FONKHAUNASHU: What? [*retreats toward* SERGEANT *who steps aside*] What's the meaning of this? I thought you needed relief? Sergeant, quick!

[*as* FONKHAUNASHU *continues the backward movement, visibly trembling,* MARIYA *removes her head scarf and her hair falls about her face in a dishevelled bunch — the effect should be one of eerie intimidation especially when her voice sounds shrilly distant and hollow. In slow motions she wraps the scarf into a* nikad *head-pad and surveys* FONKHAUNASHU *with dull, dilating eyes; lifts her right leg with amazing ease, performs ritual of passing* nikad *between her thighs, in front and behind; does three rotations over her head, pauses and applies three jets of spittle to it and ululates the* aghaa *song: she is staring at* FONKHAUNASHU *blankly and again begins the slow walk toward him with stretched-out arms; throws head-pad at* FONKHAUNASHU's *slowly retreating figure, which becomes fixed to the spot*]

62

MARIYA: Sacrifice of woman, sacrifice of the womb, you blighted child, this is your fruitful bonus! May you turn away from light and stare at the darkness of your joy! [*turns on the others*] And you staring at me, expecting me to cleanse your shit from childhood to old age, and then mourn over your unmarked tombs; but always pushing me to the side, speak now, what's my crime at this hour of uncertain passage? What's my crime at the threshold of life and death? What's my crime at this moment of transition, the silence between life and death? [*silence*] I say speak or I fix you too?

DOCKINTA: We're not the ones, mother; blame especially our book-sisters who've betrayed their constituency. We only manipulate tensions between them.

MARIYA: Ha! Shameless son, you admit to sowing confusion amongst their ranks in order to snatch their yam, having broken their veil before time? Remember, the person who fans the flames that ignite war is worse than the fighters who kill and loot and plunder.

MAN: [*tentative*] Mariya?

MARIYA: Yes, naughty son of my tears and blood? I shall not always be there for you as an abandoned piece of contingency! Mark my word!

[*lights gradually become intense and* MARIYA *recoils from the tranced performance, becomes weak as before; clutches stomach, about to collapse — at the same time that* FONKHAUNASHU *crumbles to the floor in a heap. The*

63

men, suddenly free too, rush to MARIYA*'s assistance, gentl*
lay her on the floor and rub her temples]

MAN: Mariya … please!

DOCKINTA: Those who suffer neglect and exploitatior
scheme vengeance in their pain.

SERGEANT: [*recovering*] You think so, Sah?

DOCKINTA: I don't have to think, Sergeant; I know! Bu
now is the moment for a rescue mission, and you
know the drill.

SERGENT: Mission for rescue what, Sah?

DOCKINTA: [*indicates* MARIYA] This passage to the future
and the dreams that we still dream.

MBANISAH: But he's only a man of action and...

DOCKINTA: Nonsense! Don't we all improvise in
moment of crisis? Okay, now [*to* MAN] You take care
of her for a while. [*to* SEARGENT *and* MBANISAH
Help me with this stretcher.

[*he should be talking even as he rips off cloth from the table
flings it to the floor and begins to twist the legs off, talking t
the others in spasm, when they cue in; beginning wit*
SERGENT, *who holds the table at an angle fo*
DOCKINTA *to manipulate the legs. In the meantime*
MBANISAH *suddenly gets inspired, picks up the cloth an*

64

folds it into a neat pillow, which he places at an appropriate spot on the surface of the table, now placed parallel to MARIYA. *The men lift her onto it gently; she is moaning and shivering.* SERGEANT *looks around as if confused, then quickly pulls off his jacket and covers her.*]

So much talk of nation-building ... after so many decades .... always talk, and more talk ... and when you begin to ... to doubt ... yes, that's okay ... they call you Thomas ... there, tilt and pull now ... good ... how do you build a ... a nation that's at the same time ... a piece of cake, eh? ... every conception ... pregnancy ... is a riddle of expec .... tation ... Fine ... fine. Now be gentle with her ... gently ... her arm ... yes ... That's good of you, and thoughtful too. Let's go!

MBANISAH: [*gestures at the crumbled* FONKHAUNASHU] What about him?

DOCKINTA: [*nods at* SERGEANT] He'll come back for him, after which the people will be ready to pass judgement. [*gathers masks into his bag, slings it over his shoulder. Picks up* FONKHAUNASHU's *suitcase, places it at* MARIYA's *feet, talking all the time*] Indeed, when all is said and done, blessed are still those who suffer and smile in their suffering; they shall inherit a bottomless treasury. I tell you truly, whatever verdict is passed, remember that the good men and women of this land have failed her, I mean the religious, intellectual, and political midwives, thrown away the cross of her destiny. [*to audience, with a stern stare*] But you who sit and munch and gulp, and then sleep and snore, believing in pipedreams, what lore shall you tell your children about the greyer days of their future, given the way things are? Ah, talk of complacent slaves as patriots who participate in their own enslavement! [*to the men, angrily*] Let's go now!

[*they lift the stretcher a bit clumsily and then adjust its weight to their steps, in sync, and walk out*]

-END-